21st Century Skills Library

COOL SCIENCE CAREERS

CRIME SCENE INVESTIGATOR

Tamra Orr

Cherry Lake Publishing
Ann Arbor, Michigan

363.25
Orr

Published in the United States of America by Cherry Lake Publishing
Ann Arbor, MI
www.cherrylakepublishing.com

Photo Credits: Page 6, © Bettmann/Corbis;

Library of Congress Cataloging-in-Publication Data
Orr, Tamra.
  Crime scene investigator / by Tamra Orr.
    p. cm. — (Cool science careers)
  Includes bibliographical references and index.
  ISBN-13: 978-1-60279-057-5 (hardcover : alk. paper)   978-1-60279-079-7 (pbk.)
  ISBN-10: 1-60279-057-4 (hardcover : alk. paper)   1-60279-079-5 (pbk.)
  1. Criminal investigation—Juvenile literature. 2. Crime scenes—Juvenile
literature. 3. Crime scene searches—Juvenile literature. I. Title. II.
Series.
  HV8073.8.O76 2008
  363.25'2—dc22   2007005680

Cherry Lake Publishing would like to acknowledge the work of
The Partnership for 21st Century Skills.
Please visit www.21stcenturyskills.org *for more information.*

TABLE OF CONTENTS

CHAPTER ONE

DNA and Dotson   4

CHAPTER TWO

Entering the Crime Scene   9

CHAPTER THREE

Searching for Clues   15

CHAPTER FOUR

Applying the Equipment   21

CHAPTER FIVE

Looking into the Future   25

Glossary   30

For More Information   31

Index   32

DNA and Dotson

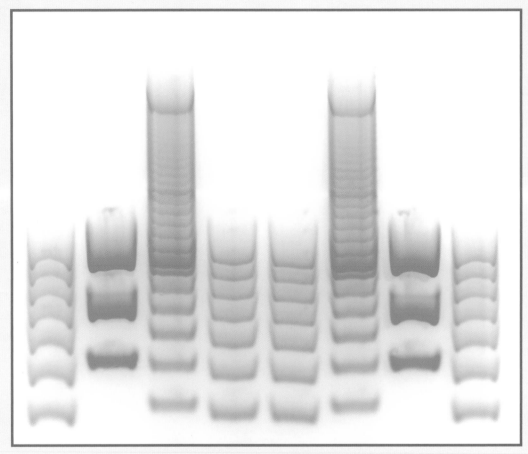

Alec Jeffreys changed criminal justice with his insights about how DNA (as seen above) could be used to distinguish a specific individual.

Throughout history, scientists have worked hard to prove various

theories through endless experiments. However, some of the world's most important discoveries are those that happened accidentally. This was certainly the case for Professor Alec Jeffreys in 1984. In the early morning of September 15, he actually experienced one of those rare and profound "Eureka!" moments.

A New Perspective

Jeffreys had been working on **DNA** (deoxyribonucleic acid) for years. He and his team studied the differences in people's DNA patterns in hopes that the information could be used to help cure some diseases. This time, however, Jeffreys had a new idea. DNA could do more than just point out diseases. DNA could be used to prove a person's identity!

21st Century Content

Your DNA is found everywhere in your body! It's in your hair, skin, fingernails, blood, saliva, and bones. Once a person's DNA information is placed in a database, doctors, scientists, or crime scene investigators anywhere in the world can match it to a sample.

*Gary Dotson served eight years in an Illinois jail before
DNA evidence helped prove he was innocent.*

DNA Fingerprinting

Jeffreys and his team improved the process of identifying a person

through DNA. Soon, the professor was being asked to help solve crimes

that had the police baffled. By looking at the DNA evidence at a crime

scene, he helped determine who had committed the crime. In 1986,

DNA evidence from clothing or elsewhere must be carefully preserved away from heat and humidity, which may destroy it.

however, Jeffreys's DNA research did something different: it helped prove a

man was innocent. His name was Gary Dotson. He was in prison.

The Accusation

It had begun in 1977. A police officer stumbled across 16-year-old

Cathleen Crowell. Her clothes were dirty and torn. She was in tears. She

said she had been kidnapped and attacked by three young men. She was taken to the hospital, and samples of hair and other substances were collected. Later, Crowell picked Dotson's picture out of a group of possible suspects.

DNA Proves the Truth

At the trial, Crowell insisted Dotson was the man who had hurt her. Dotson was convicted and sentenced to many years in prison. Three years later, Crowell admitted that she had lied, and experts turned to DNA for an answer. It proved that Dotson was not guilty. He was one of the first people in the world to be proven innocent through the use of DNA.

CHAPTER TWO

ENTERING THE CRIME SCENE

*Early in any investigation, police officers block off
the crime scene so that evidence can be collected.*

You have often watched the scene on television. A crime has been

committed. Yellow tape is put up to keep onlookers from entering the area.

People with specialized tool kits arrive in official vehicles. Everyone gets

*Some large police departments use special vans and trucks
to bring forensic tools to the scene of a crime.*

out of the way to let them through. The crime

scene investigators are here. The search for evidence

can begin!

Getting Organized

Crime scene investigators are called to many

kinds of situations, including **homicides,** assaults,

armed robberies, home invasions, and burglaries. It is

their job to do several very important things:

- interview

- examine

- photograph

- sketch

- process

If you regularly watch the nightly news, you hear stories of murder. Yet the U.S. is not near the top of the list for most murders per capita (for the population). That sad distinction belongs to Colombia, South Africa, Jamaica, Venezuela, and Russia. (2003 figures)

Life & Career Skills

What kind of personal traits would be good to have for each of these jobs?

Crime scene investigators often work in teams. A team usually includes a leader, a photographer, a sketcher, an evidence recorder, and perhaps one or two other specialists. Team leaders decide what needs to be done. They make sure the scene is secure so evidence cannot be **contaminated**. Photographers take pictures of everything in the area. Sketchers draw detailed pictures of people involved in the crime. Evidence recorders describe every clue they find in a special **log,** or journal.

The Rest of the Team

Even more specialists may be needed sometimes. A bomb technician

will be called if there is some kind of explosive. In a murder case,

entomologists may be asked to study bugs and help settle the question of

how long a person has been dead.

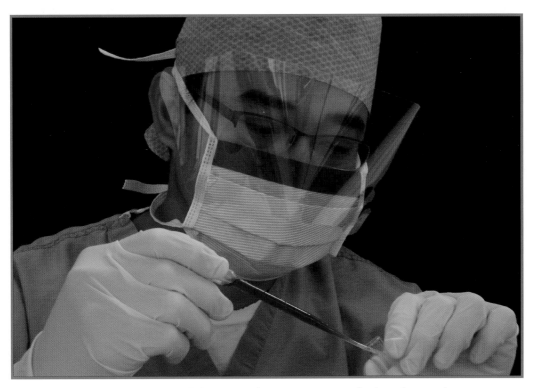

Besides sometimes helping to solve crimes, entomologists often study
insects that cause such diseases as malaria and West Nile Virus.

Piles of Paperwork

No matter what kind of responsibility a specific crime scene

investigator has, it involves a lot of paperwork. Every crime requires a

worksheet with clear, detailed

descriptions of what happened, a

photo log of every picture taken,

multiple sketches and diagrams

for reference, and evidence record

logs that list every clue. All of these

details will be needed later when

the **forensic** department begins

piecing the crime together.

*Crime scene investigators must be
meticulous about paperwork so their
results will withstand challenges in court.*

CHAPTER THREE

SEARCHING FOR CLUES

*Evidence collection at a crime scene is an
everyday task for crime scene investigators.*

Some evidence at a crime scene is huge. You can't miss a mangled car

or a burned building. What about a muddy footprint or torn fingernail,

however? How hard is it to spot a mysterious fiber or scrap of hair? They

Learning & Innovation Skills

If any part of the crime took place outside, the search must be completed there before Mother Nature can ruin the evidence. How could wind, rain, or snow damage evidence?

could provide clues, so they have to be discovered and analyzed. Because of this, investigating teams choose from a variety of search patterns. This helps to ensure that nothing is missed.

Picking a Pattern

Investigators often search a crime scene in a pattern to ensure it is thoroughly covered. They may choose an inward spiral, starting at the outside of the scene and working inward. They can also start at the center and work out. Another option is the grid pattern, where investigators walk in parallel lines from one side to the other. Finally, they may use the zone method, where each investigator is assigned a specific section to examine.

*The body of a crime victim may be covered
partly to protect any evidence on it.*

In a murder investigation, investigators look at several things before the

body is removed from the crime scene.

- Are there marks or stains on the clothing?

- Are there obvious injuries to the body? What do these tell about the

  cause of death?

Life & Career Skills

What role do ethics play in the job of crime scene investigator? What kind of responsibility is being assumed with this type of work?

- Is there blood? If so, what does its pattern tell about what happened? If not, why?

All Shapes and Sizes

Evidence comes in all shapes and sizes, and investigators know not to overlook anything. Some of the most common items they study are:

- blood (wet, dry, from victim, from suspect, patterns)

- other bodily liquids (saliva, vomit, etc.)

- hair

- fibers and threads

- glass pieces (from windows, bottles, and pictures)

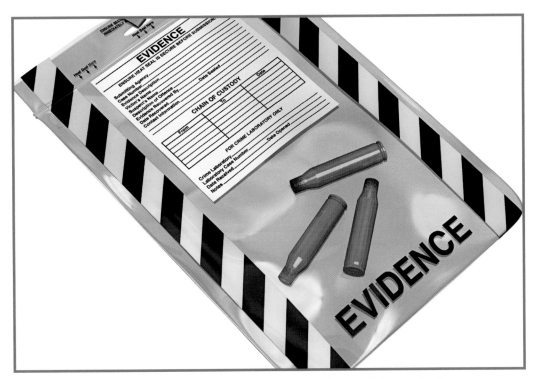

Evidence bags often have labels attached to them to help standardize the information and make sure nothing important is left out.

- paint chips

- prints (from hands, fingers, toes, feet, shoes, and tires)

- soil samples

- weapons

Learning & Innovation Skills

Why is it important to carefully label each piece of evidence and keep it separate from other things found at the crime scene?

Preserving the Evidence

Keeping evidence safe is just as important as finding it. To do this, investigators use multiple sizes and types of plastic and paper bags and containers along with airtight metal cans. Each piece of evidence—from something as large as a murder weapon to the smallest blood sample—is put into a separate container. Next, each container is labeled with the date, time, and location where its contents was found.

CHAPTER FOUR

APPLYING THE EQUIPMENT

*Reliable photographic equipment is essential
for good documentation of a crime scene.*

Every profession has its own tools of the trade. Of course, crime scene

investigators do, too. For a crime scene photographer, typical equipment

includes several cameras, lots of film, extra batteries, lenses, filters, flashes,

and a tripod.

Finding Fingerprints

Fingerprint experts use several brushes and kinds of powder along with tape, lift cards, and a magnifying glass. They look for prints on clothing, doors, furniture, and other surfaces. These "fingerprints" can come from fingers but also from hands, toes, and feet.

Latent fingerprints are the most common. They are caused when dirt, sweat, or other residue is pushed onto another object. They can be left on objects such as mirrors, glass, paper, and clothing.

An investigator who collects blood samples carries sterile cloth, glass microscope slides, distilled water, a scalpel, tweezers, and scissors. Other investigators specialize in making casts of footprints. They carry a special powder as well as a bowl and a rubber spatula for mixing it up with water. Along with footprints, this investigator may take a cast of tire tracks from the vehicles that have been in the area.

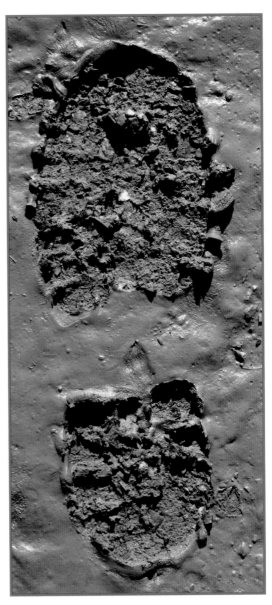

A shoe print can help determine a shoe size, whether the shoe is for women or men, or even a specific pair of shoes!

Life & Career Skills

Each person's job at a crime scene dictates the kind of equipment he or she will use. Why would patience and thoroughness be good qualities for all of these jobs?

Investigators preserve evidence in plastic and paper bags, glass vials, and metal cans. They also need a flashlight, clipboard for paperwork, pens, a compass, chalk, and police tape. Sometimes they use hammers, screwdrivers, wrenches, shovels, and wire cutters, too.

Special investigators are called to crime scenes with a **biohazard**. They wear sterile suits and disposable gloves, booties, face masks, and aprons. Extra precautions must be taken. These specialists follow the rules!

CHAPTER FIVE

LOOKING INTO THE FUTURE

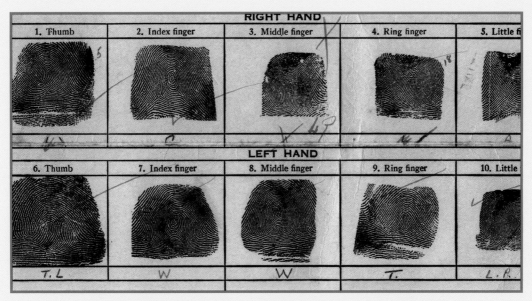

Fingerprints were once the best tool to determine who committed a crime, but newer tools such as DNA analysis are much more reliable.

Crime scene investigation has come a long way since 1776. Paul Revere identified the corpse of General Warren that year by a false tooth Revere had made for him out of a walrus tusk.

What might happen in the future to change crime scene investigation? Will it look anything like the science fiction movies with robots fighting

battles as in *Robocop* or stopping a crime before it happens as in *Minority Report*?

In some ways, the future is already here. Robots are being used to handle potentially explosive devices. One day they may be used for finding hidden, armed suspects without risking the lives of police officers or others.

Computers have already sped up the search process for many police departments. Computers can connect distant investigators to each other. They can also link investigators to the National Fingerprint File and the National DNA Database.

We Know Who You Are

DNA has helped make the identification of individual people much faster and easier. Other techniques are becoming even more popular. Devices that scan the **iris** of your eye are already used in some high security areas. Fingerprint readers that electronically scan fingerprint patterns and **digitize** them are being used more often. Some experts even believe that a specific type of odor detector will someday be used to track a suspect like a bloodhound can.

Can You See Me Now?

One technique that may help crime scene investigators is the growing use of **surveillance** cameras

Learning & Innovation Skills

Look at the bottom of the shoes you are wearing. What kind of impression would they make in the ground? What could someone tell about you by looking at the impressions?

*Surveillance cameras are now in wide use around the world.
London, England, alone has more than 4 million of them!*

in major American cities. Electronic security more than doubled between

2000 and 2005. Such security was once video-based. However, new "smart

cameras" now use computer software. The cameras can hear a gunshot,

spot an illegally parked car, or monitor someone behaving oddly. However, some people object to the use of these cameras. They say their right to privacy is being violated.

The Real Heroes

There is a reason that shows such as *CSI* are so popular. Many people are fascinated by crime scenes and the mysteries they can present. Real life crime-scene investigators are the heroes in these stories, both on screen and off. Their dedication, time, skills, and education help to take the questions out of the crime and provide the solutions instead.

Crime scene investigations are shown regularly on television. What kinds of elements might be changed from reality to suit the needs of TV? How do you think this fact influences what the public thinks about crime scene investigations?

Glossary

biohazard (BAHY-oh-haz-erd) a biological agent that constitutes a threat to humans

contaminated (kuhn-TAM-uh-neyt-ed) impure or unsuitable through contact with something else

DNA (dee en ay) deoxyribonucleic acid, a main component of genetics

digitize (DIJ-i-tahyz) convert to digital form for use on a computer

entomologist (en-tuh-MOL-uh-jist) scientist who studies bugs and insects

forensic (fuh-REN-sik) connected with and/or used in courts of law

homicide (HOM-uh-sahyd) murder

iris (AHY-ris) the colored portion of an eye

latent (LEYT-nt) present but not readily visible or evident

log (lawg) journal or reporting book

surveillance (ser-VEY-luhns) watch kept over a person or group

FOR MORE INFORMATION:

Books

Allman, Toney. *Crime Scene Investigations—The Medical Examiner.* San Diego: Lucent Books, 2006.

Bowers, Vivien. *Crime Scene: How Investigators Use Science to Track Down the Bad Guys.* Toronto: Maple Tree Press, 2006.

Harris, Elizabeth Snoke. *Crime Scene Science Fair Projects.* New York: Lark Books, 2006.

Schulz, Karen, *Crime Scene Detective: Using Science and Critical Thinking to Solve Crimes.* Austin, TX: Prufrock Press, 2005.

Yancey, Diane. *Crime Scene Investigations—Murder.* San Diego: Lucent Books, 2006.

Other Media

http://www.nifs.com.au/F_S_A/FSA_frame.html?Student_Information. asp&1 is a good site to find out about forensic science in Australia.

http://www.interpol.int/default.asp is the home page for Interpol, the world's largest international police organization.

http://www.crimezzz.net/forensic_history/index.htm is a time line of forensic science events and people.

INDEX

armed robberies, 11
assaults, 11

biohazards, 24
blood samples, 18, 22, 23
bomb technician, 13
burglaries, 11

computers, 26
contaminated evidence, 12
crime scene, 9, 11
crime scene investigators
    future of, 25–29
    jobs of, 11–12
    paperwork, 14
    work hours, 22

Colombia, 11
crime scene security, 12
CSI television show, 29

digitize, 27
DNA (doxyribonucleic acid)
    DNA fingerprinting, 6
    identification and, 5–9, 27
Dotson, Gary, 6–8

entomologists, 13
equipment
    biohazards, 24
    blood sample collection, 23
    computers, 26

fingerprinting equipment,
    22, 27
photographer's equipment,
    21
preserving evidence, 24
robots, 26
evidence
    biohazards, 24
    contaminated evidence, 12
    pattern search, 16
    preserving evidence, 20,
        24
    types of, 15–19
evidence log, 12, 14
evidence recorders, 12

fingerprints, 22, 27
footprints, 23
forensic department, 14

home invasions, 11
homicides, 11, 17

identification, 5–9, 25, 27

Jamaica, 11
Jeffreys, Alec, 4–7

logs, 12, 14

Minority Report, 26

National DNA Database, 26

National Fingerprint File, 26

photographers, 12
    crime scene photography,
        12, 21
    photo log, 14
    surveillance cameras, 27–
        29
South Africa, 11

Revere, Paul, 25
Robocop, 26
robots, 26
Russia, 11

sketchers, 12
surveillance cameras, 27–29

Venezuela, 11

ABOUT THE AUTHOR

Tamra Orr is a full-time writer and author living in the gorgeous Pacific Northwest. She loves her job because she learns more about the world every single day and then turns that information into pop quizzes for her patient and tolerant children (ages 16, 13, and 10). She has written more than 80 nonfiction books for people of all ages, so she never runs out of material and is sure she'd be a champion on Jeopardy!